ANN WEEMS

From Advent's Alleluia
to Easter's Morning Light

Poetry for Worship, Study, and Devotion

WESTMINSTER
JOHN KNOX PRESS
LOUISVILLE · KENTUCKY

First edition
Published by Westminster John Knox Press
Louisville, Kentucky

11 12 13 14 15 16 17 18 19—10 9 8 7 6 5 4 3 2

Scripture quotations from the New Revised Standard Version of the Bible are copyright © 1989 by the Division of Christian Education of the National Council of the Churches of Christ in the U.S.A. and are used by permission.

Book design by Drew Stevens

Library of Congress Cataloging-in-Publication Data

Weems, Ann, 1934–
   From Advent's alleluia to Easter's morning light : poetry for worship, study, and devotion / by Ann Weems.
     p. cm.
   ISBN 978-0-664-23491-1 (alk. paper)
   1. Christian poetry, American. I. Title.
   PS3573.E354F76 2010
   811'.54—dc22

                        2010003127

PRINTED IN THE UNITED STATES OF AMERICA

To Stuart, my December Angel,

Love you forever!

—Mom

Contents

Acknowledgments

I feel about acknowledgments the same way I felt when I was a child and finished my prayers with "and everybody in the whole wide world." In my case there are always so many to thank!

I am extremely grateful for the work of the Staff at Westminster John Knox Press. Thanks to David Dobson, Dan Braden, and Emily Kiefer, not only for their expertise, but for their patience and their thoroughness and their kindness! And a big applause also to those who work with David and Dan and Emily. I appreciate you all so very much! The production of a book is a beautiful thing. Years of thanks to Annie McClure, who gives in such a willing, competent, and engaging way and always has the answers. And to Robin Howell, who graciously takes the work off of my desk when it comes to permissions.

Smiles and thanks to my family and friends who accept that I can't be disturbed when I'm writing, but love me still!

And, dear readers, a big bouquet of thank-yous to all of you who are so faithful to my writing, you who invite me to speak, who come and listen, who take my poetry and create worship and paintings and weavings and music and sculpture, and joy, to those who speak to me heart to heart, perhaps even soul to soul.

Thanks to all of you from the bottom of my heart for the generosity of your spirits!

I want to express my deepest gratitude for Stephanie Egnotovich, dear editor and dear friend through the years. Fortunately, she knew how very much I appreciated her and a few weeks before her death she thanked me once again for the books I have written. She is now my Angel Editor.

Ann Weems

Introduction

John 1:1–5

> In the beginning was the Word, and the Word was with God, and the Word was God. He was in the beginning with God. All things came into being through him, and without him not one thing came into being. What has come into being in him was life, and the life was the light of all people. The light shines in the darkness, and the darkness did not overcome it.

I imagine a theologian could spend a lifetime on that one text. The more I read it the more I find to think about, to write about. This book is about the Word incarnate, God coming to live in this world, in our world. Sometimes, however, I feel as though we are trying to create Christ by consensus.

We in the Church seem to go
> from professing the Word
> to easily digressing from the Word.
> Let us together try to find
> the eyes to see and the ears to hear
> Jesus, this Word of God,
> as he speaks to us about who he is.
> Perhaps then we can begin to return
> to confessing the Word
> and to joyfully living in the blessing of the Word.

There is another text that I want to emphasize. Jesus asked his disciples who people say that he is, and they had various answers. But then Jesus asked them, "But who do you say that I am?" And Peter answered, "You are the Messiah" (Matt. 16:13–20).

My hope is that the reader will print out (or type in large type) these two texts and refer to them throughout the reading of this book.

In a previous book, *Putting the Amazing Back in Grace*, I also spoke in that introduction about the Matthew Scripture (which appears also in other Gospels). It is a haunting text, and I have it on a sticky note on my computer so as I write I won't forget that Jesus asks this question of all of us: Who do you say that I am?

Couple the two texts together, and look at the words of the Word and hear Jesus tell us over and over who he is. It's these texts that I am enfolding into the biblical stories I've chosen to help us find our answers.

The poems in this book are written to be used in worship, in personal devotions, and in discussions (hopefully lively ones!). They are biblically based; therefore, one cannot discuss the poems without engaging in a Bible study. My hope is that the poems will make it easier to contribute to the discussion. My hope is that we in the church will think deeply about who we are and what we say we believe. My hope is that we in the church will continue to question ourselves about our discipleship, answering Jesus as he asks, "Who do you say that I am?"

Before We Speak about the Word of God

Through all the words, O God, may it be
your Word that is heard.
In the name of Jesus, we pray. Amen.

Pre-Advent

One More Wall, One More Olive Tree

One more wall in a walled-in world.
One more wall in a walled-out world.
Keep bombs out. Keep tanks out.
Keep people out . . . or is it in?

Two women, divided by wall,
make their way to each other,
the tall, thin Palestinian waving her ID
to the Israeli border guard who nods her through.
Beyond the wall, she strides toward the café
where the Israeli woman sits, waits.
Eyes like stars in a black field,
Sarah is striking in spite of white hair.
She motions for Hagar to sit.
Shalom, Mother of my firstborn!
Hagar smiles, Salaam, Sarah who cradled me
in your arms as I birthed our son, Ishmael.
Unspoken memories bring laughter.
Hagar speaks: It wasn't funny then,
you who laugh even at God.
Sarah agrees, No, and it isn't funny now.
I laugh at our childishness, not at our faithlessness.
Were that we had been *childlike,* Hagar muses.
Would that I had learned a lesson
from our sons at play! Sarah replies.
We both remember my unmerciful taunting! says Hagar.
Sarah's starry eyes mist.
It took me so long to believe God's word! So long!
Hagar leans closer:

Even though we were jealous and cruel,
God saw our tears and heard our hearts
and forgave.
And kept promises, Sarah adds.
Hagar agreed, You *did* give birth to laughter!
Sarah laughs once more; and God *did* hear Ishmael.
God kept promises of land and heir!
But have the nations been blessed? Hagar asks.
The land lies red as our heirs
continue to kill one another!
Daily danger, says Sarah.
Perhaps our story is not heard.
It's not about our scandalous behavior.
It's about not believing God's promises:
God's story is the scandalous one!
That God would keep these promises!
that when the promises are in jeopardy,
that God would provide!
Even now.

Even now, Hagar repeats.
She rises. It's time.
Together, they make their way to
the group who awaits them,
Palestinians and Israelis meeting
for Friday prayers.
Welcome, Mothers!
Kneeling together in the midst
of these kneeling children of God,
Hagar and Sarah plant an olive tree,
their hands patting the rich God-given earth.

On their knees, on promised land with promised heirs,
they pray for peace, one less wall, far more olive trees.
Even in the choked voices of grief and despair,
  the group prays.
Sarah turns her starry eyes to God's sky and counts.
Is anything too hard for God? she asks.

To Sarah, to Hagar, and to us
in the midst of our own barren wandering,
O God, provide land and heir and blessing,
a blessing for all the nations of the earth,
a blessing of peace.

This Time Around

This time around,
Miriam's tambourine
lies on the shelf.
Her feet aren't dancing.
There is no music.

This time around,
Miriam's singing
is not heard.
Her voice is stilled.
There is no joy.

This time around,
no Song of the Sea;
both sides drowning
in the river of blood
this time around.

Miriam, do you call for worship?
She shakes her head.
Ears don't hear
through blasts of warfare
this time around.

Eyes can't see through
bloodstained glasses;
voices can't speak
choked on tears
this time around.

Shackles of fear,
chains of mistrust,
bonds of grief . . .
this time around,
all are slaves.

And still it comes
this flood of hatred,
these waters of revenge.
Is there no hope
this time around?

This time around
stones are hurled
terrorists bomb
the innocent die
this time around.

This time around
tanks roll
guns kill
the innocent die
this time around.

Miriam asks beneath
the palm of Deborah:
Minister of War,
when will it stop?
Deborah weeps.

Pray for me,
Priest of God,

Pray for me,
Deborah cries.
Pray for us all!

Beneath the
palm of Deborah,
Priest and Minister
kneel in prayer
this time around.

No songs of triumph
in their hearts,
they cry to God,
not for victory,
but for peace.

Praying the words,
Miriam remembers
horse and rider
drowned in the sea.
This time around, she weeps.

Praying the words,
Deborah remembers
Sisera's mother awaiting
her son, already killed.
This time around, she weeps.

This time around
God's voice is heard:
How can you sing when
my children are drowning?
God weeps, too.

The obscenity of war
has carved its knife into the
spirit of the people of God.
They no longer dance
this time around.

War after war,
generation after generation
of hardened hearts . . .
The prophets ask:
Where are the hearts that sing?

This time around
Miriam and Deborah
cannot sing, cannot shout,
cannot celebrate
this time around.

Sing, Miriam, sing!
Shout, Deborah, shout!
Is your God not here?
Does your God not hear?
This time around?

Kneeling, they give thanks
for one child saved,
and in that there is hope
that God is still here
this time around.

Kneeling, they pray
to God who
taught them Peace

from the very beginning . . .
and even this time around.

They kneel and pray,
not for victory, but for peace,
for this time around
they know that peace
is the only victory.

Jerusalem, Jerusalem,
Lift up your hearts and sing!
Sing, Miriam! Shout, Deborah!
O Little Town of Bethlehem,
where are your tambourines?

Return to Bethlehem

Widowed women,
weary from the dying,
find little solace from a world
that casually cries, "Move on!"
No more time for weeping.
Naomi's husband gone,
her sons gone.
Their wives widowed.
No grandchildren.
Nothing.
Where is her God?

How different when Naomi
first saw New York!
Delegate to the UN,
Elimelech provided
privilege and plenty.
Mahlon married Ruth,
a translator at the UN.
Chilion married Orpah,
who worked at MoMA.
How God had blessed Naomi then!

Now Naomi knew her only hope
was in returning to Bethlehem
and selling their land.
I'll go wherever you go, insisted Ruth.
Your people will be my people.
Your God will be my God.

Back in Bethlehem,
Naomi said her name was Bitter.
And why not?
No husband, no son, no home.
Bethlehem enmeshed in war.
God had forgotten her name.

Naomi waved as Ruth left
that morning.
At the end of the day,
Ruth had a government job.
Overqualified, yes, but for
now filing work was fine.
Ruth and Naomi could eat.

For whom will you work?
Boaz, Ruth answered.
My cousin, Naomi said,
a very wealthy and
important man in Israel.
His work is negotiation,
negotiation with our enemies.
His work is never done.

Naomi said, Tonight give thanks,
for God has blessed you.
Tomorrow I will tell you
what to do.

Ruth wore perfume, and the rose blouse,
and said to Boaz, as Naomi had told her:
I like very much working with you.
He took her to lunch at Saul's Café.

By lunch the next day,
all had been decided.
Boaz bought Naomi's land.
Ruth lost her filing job and
became a translator working
with Boaz in government
negotiations for peace.
Ruth didn't have to be told
to thank God.

After the wedding and
after the birth of Obed,
Naomi's friends said
Ruth was worth seven sons.
Naomi held the child,
the son finally given to her,
and gave thanks to God
who had kept covenant.

. . . .

Theologians say it is a pleasant tale.
How pleasant could it have been
for the widows?
No husbands, no money, no heirs.
"Powerless," in the world's eyes,
powerless, not pleasant!
I suppose the pleasant part began
when Boaz "redeemed" them,
or was it the women
who redeemed the nation?
The story ends with a twist,
for Ruth turns out to be the
great-grandmother of David.

And eventually in that lineage,
in that little town of Bethlehem,
Jesus, the Redeemer, is born.
Jesus in the lineage
of a Gentile woman.
Birth to the barren.
Power to the powerless.
God had heard Naomi.
Pleasant tale or
profound prophecy?

Hannah at Prayer

Hannah's mother said she wasn't eating well.
Her mother-in-law said, Take vitamins.
Her friends told her to go to a fertility clinic.
Her sister told her to go to a psychiatrist.
Her husband asked her why she couldn't be content
    with him.
His ex-wife said, I've already given Elkanah plenty
    of sons!
Only her grandmother said, Keep praying, Hannah.
God will hear you.
She told her grandmother that she would continue
    to pray.
Still no pregnancy.

When the Holy Days came, Hannah and Elkanah
went to the synagogue in St. Louis to give thanks.
Hannah gave thanks, but asked God to give her a son.
I'm miserable! she said. Nervous and stressed!
Please remember me and hear my prayer.
Elkanah went to a family reunion with his children,
but Hannah remained in the synagogue.
The more she prayed the more she cried.
Please, God, give me a son. I promise to dedicate him
    to you.
He will grow up serving you, and live with you always.
O God, please hear Hannah at prayer.
She prayed in silence, but she wept loudly.
She made so much noise in her weeping
that the rabbi came to see what was going on.

He had been having trouble with street people
who came to find sanctuary and food.
This woman must be drunk, or is she mentally ill?
He didn't know whether to call a doctor or the police.
Hannah saw him and said, Please pray for me.
When he saw she was harmless, and fervently at prayer,
the rabbi said, Go in peace. May the God of Israel
grant the petition you have made.
Hannah and Elkanah returned home.
God remembered Hannah at prayer.
When the child came, Hannah named him Samuel,
"I have asked him of the Lord."

Hannah kept her side of the covenant
and gave the child to the Lord, praying:
"My heart exults in the LORD;
my strength is exalted in my God."
. . . for "the barren has borne seven."

Once again the barren one gives birth.
Once again the impossible is made possible.
Once again, God heard his faithful at prayer.
Once again we understand that prayer is
an action, an act of faith.
Hannah and God kept covenant.

The Word of God

In the beginning was the Word, and the Word was
with God, and the Word was God. . . . All things were
made through the Word, and without the Word was not
anything made that was made.

In a wave of wonder,
in an extravaganza of imagination,
in a roar of deafening waters,
in a drum roll of thunder,
God said let there be Light!
and the dazzling sun of Day
made her entrance,
singing her song of Life.
Then in a stunning display of fireworks,
lightning leaping in bolts,
stars hurling through ink black sky,
moon floating above,
the Light of Night took her bow.
The stage was set.
Right from the beginning
the Word was there,
with God.
The Word was God.
And without the Word not anything
was made that was made.
Day and Night,
darkness and light,
waters and land,
trees and living plants,
animals and birds,

and people,
all created by God.
Right from the beginning
the Word of God
was spoken in miracles.
Right from the beginning,
in the light of God's love,
the people of God
were created for
covenant keeping.
I will be your God
and you will be my people.
Right from the beginning
the Word was Love
and the Word was Light
and the Word was Life.
Right from the beginning
God's people were invited
to walk in the way of the Word.
God saw that it was good.
It was very good.

Until, that is, somebody
left the door open in paradise,
and Death walked on stage
and turned off the light.
Somebody or somebodies thought
they didn't have to listen to God,
thought they didn't need
to keep covenant.
Call them by whatever
names you like:
Adam, Eve, the neighborhood snake;

it's all the same.
God's people had been entrusted
with earth and stars
and all living things,
and yet it wasn't enough.
Something gnawed away
at the souls of God's people
and they broke covenant . . .
right there in the beginning . . .
and again . . .
       and again . . .
             and again.

Somebody or somebodies
wanted to be in charge.
Somebody or somebodies
wanted to be God's favorite.
Somebody or somebodies
wanted to be God.
Somebody or somebodies
didn't like the diversity.
They wanted everybody
to be like they were.

Killing was born
and hatred
and greed
and deception
and suspicion
and hard-heartedness
and mean-spiritedness
and distrust
and power grabbing

and jealousy
and prejudice.
The people of God
had chosen Death
instead of Life.
God was grieved
to the heart.

Return to me, God said.
Over and over and over again
Return to me.
God sent prophets
to tell the people
to return to God,
but just as Cain hated Abel,
the people in the world
hated each other
and wars began
and God's people
still would not return,
return to covenant living
return to the way of life
that God had offered.
God asked for justice
and mercy and
humbleness,
but the people of the world
wanted justice for themselves
and mercy for themselves
and anything but humbleness.
God had promised not
to send another flood.
Besides God loved the people still

even though they walked in darkness,
so God sent a great Light,
the Word of God Incarnate.

We know the story.
Even though God kept covenant
on behalf of the people,
even though Jesus walked on this earth,
even though he is the Way, the Truth,
and the life,
the world knew him not.
We know the story.
The people didn't want
to share their bread and their wine.
The people didn't want
to love one another.
And so they crucified
the only One who was Love.
The angels wept.

But still God loved the people.
And forgave them.
Jesus was resurrected.
And the Holy Spirit was sent
to guide the church of Jesus Christ.

Why then is the world today
in such darkness?
Why do we open our newspapers
and read stories and see photos
of the manifestations of hatred?
Why does blood cover our TVs?
Why are the sick not healed?

Why are the poor not fed?
not housed?
Why are children abused?
Why are the weak exploited?
On and on and on . . .
Terror and violence . . .
Where is the Church of Jesus Christ?

It's about Jesus. . . .
It's always been about Jesus.
In the beginning was the Word
and the Word was with God
and the Word was God
But the world has a way
of creating God in its own image.
When we don't like
the Word of God,
we dilute the gospel
into something insignificant.
We begin making more rules.
We write lists of what
we're going to do
in the future.
The Word of God
is far more dangerous
than that.
The Word of God
changes our lives.
It changes our lives now.
Love the Lord your God
with all your heart
and all your soul
and all your mind.

Love your neighbor
as yourself.
Follow me.
Go into all the world
and preach the gospel.
Preach the good news to the poor.
Feed my sheep.
Preach Love.
Preach Peace.

I read the newspapers
about the church conventions.
We Presbyterians are not the
only ones with internal problems.
The Presbyterian Church
is worried about a significant
decrease in membership
and a significant decrease
in money.

How about the Presbyterian Church
worrying about a significant
decrease in faithfulness?!??!!
We can't find money enough
to budget some of the needed
justice and peace ministries,
but for years we've found money
to finance our quarreling,
our very costly quarreling.
Follow me.
The soul of the church
is bruised by its silence.

Something is gnawing at
the souls of the people of God.
Somewhere along the way
we thought we didn't have
to listen to the Word of God,
thought we didn't have to
walk in covenant.
Instead of keeping covenant,
we've turned off the light and
are spending our time quarreling.
How must the heart of God grieve!
How must the Good Shepherd weep!
when there are
so many of his sheep to be fed,
so many sheep lost,
so many sheep waiting
for the Church of Jesus Christ
to find them,
so many sick longing to be healed,
so many tortured waiting to be freed,
so many war plagued . . .
bleeding, homeless, hungry . . .

Death has taken center stage,
Hatred takes curtain call after curtain call.
Violence bows to the applause of the crowd,
waiting waiting waiting
for the Church of Jesus Christ
to climb into its pulpit
and preach the Word of God.
The Word of God is not War;
The Word of God is Peace.
The Word of God is not Torture;

The Word of God is Compassion.
The Word of God is not Hate;
The Word of God is Love.
Is it fear of losing more members,
more money,
that we do not stand in solidarity
with the Prince of Peace?!

Our darkness begins
where our covenant ends.
If the love of God is not
written on our hearts,
there is no covenant light,
and flailing in the dark
gets us nowhere.
The miracle is,
the stunning absurdity
of the Gospel is,
that the people of God
fell into a pit of darkness
because they didn't have the eyes
to see the light of God . . .
but our covenant God had compassion
and hearing the cries of the people,
had pity on them and forgave them.

The world was created in miracles.
Surely there are miracles
yet to come.
If the people of God
will open their hearts
to the Word of God,
they will have the eyes
to see the Light of the World.

Advent

Angels Still Appear

Angels still appear to those
ready to receive blessings
in spite of the barren
impossibility of their lives.

Elizabeth still recognizes Jesus
and calls him Lord,
receiving him to her heart,
in spite of the distraction
of her own blessing.

Blessings still come
to those who believe
that nothing is impossible
in the hand of God.

Mary still gives birth,
not just every Advent,
Mary still gives birth
each day to this Child
who advents into hearts,
unexpectedly and forever.

Herods still live who
would kill this Child,
but Mary and Joseph
still flee into the desert,
and the night,
to protect the One
given into their keeping.

Doors still slam in the
inns of this world,
Herods still plot to kill,
deserts and darkness
still threaten our safety,
but God still lives.
In spite of war and terror,
Mary gives birth
to the Prince of Peace.
In spite of hunger,
Mary gives birth
to the Bread of Life.
In spite of lost sheep,
Mary gives birth
to the Good Shepherd.
In spite of hearts
pregnant with hatred,
Mary gives birth to LOVE.

It is not done!
It is not done!
It is not done!
The birthing is not over.
The blessings continue.
Angels wait in the wings!

The Promised One, the Expected One, the Messiah

We've heard that the people of the time
had certain ideas about the Promised One,
thought the Expected One would be born in a palace
or come down from Heaven on a cloud,
never expected the Messiah
would be sent as a baby to people like Mary and Joseph. . . .
Our question is this:
What is our expectation?
What promise do we hold to our hearts?
Who is this Messiah born to us?

The One-Star Night

Into an extremely dark and bitterly cold December
came a one-star night.
Those who had compassion
found room and
were filled with wonder
at the brightness of the star above them.
Those who saw
fell to their knees in fear,
but listened to the angels' song
and ran to see.
Those who heard the baby's cry
believed,
and fell to their knees,
this time in worship.
Those who followed the star
already believed,
and knew the time was now.
They persisted in their journey
through the dark and cold,
bringing gifts to this One
born to us all
in a one-star night.

Fly!

In the early morning hours
when the world waits for Jesus,
the angels gather in great anticipation
and listen for the voice of God:
Fly!!
In tremendous fluttering
They're off.
Those of us who believe
Know it's time for us to fly, too!!

The UPS Angel

The tallest fullest tree on the lot, the man said.
Before I could object, the tree was cut,
hoisted by two men to the roof of the car,
tied securely and off we went,
driving home through the streets of St. Louis.
It seemed even taller and larger
when we got home.
My husband cut the cords;
the tree slid down the side of the car.
How on earth are we going to get it into the house?
      he asked.
We can't, I answered.
Just then a UPS truck stopped in front of the house.
A very tall man jumped out,
ran to the tree, picked it up
as though it were made of feathers,
took it through the door into the living room,
put it in the tree stand,
made sure it was safely and tightly secured,
stood up with his arms up in an almost praise position,
turned around, looking at the Christmas créches on
      the mantel.
"Wonderful! Wonderful!" he said,
and started toward the entranceway and stopped.
"Oh, the Angel Wall!" he said,
in a quiet, almost reverent voice.
"They told me about it," he said.
He stood there for a few seconds,
looking at the angels, flying on the wall.
And then we started thanking him,
my husband saying:

"God bless you!"
He smiled at us:
"And you," he said.
With that he was gone,
running down the steps,
almost flying into the truck.
We stood in the doorway,
waving.
"You realize," I said,
"that we just had a visit from an angel."

What I Want for Christmas

A miracle!
A miracle is what I want for Christmas!
A miracle!
In the early morning hours,
    people still in darkness,
I want us all to be awakened
    by the pealing of church bells
        loud and wild,
    pealing over and over and
        over again,
    urgent, joyful, overwhelmingly
        loud and wild!
And when we rush out to see
        what's going on,
    neighbors in front of us,
        neighbors behind us,
    all of us rushing to the
        church, the bells
    continue their pealing,
        loud and wild,
    and over and over again.

On the steps of the church
    stands a very tall Angel
        dressed in red, and he
            speaks to us:
    "Don't be afraid; I have great news,
        for to you is born this day
        a Savior who is Christ the Lord."

With those words there is much
        fluttering of wings
   and the sky is full of angels,
      all singing, bells still pealing,
"Glory to God in the highest
    and on earth peace and goodwill."

With that we are lifted into the
        still dark sky
   and then put down in front
      of a dazzling light.
When our eyes adjust,
   we drop to our knees,
for we are mangerside
   in front of the Holy Child,
     bells still pealing;
       angels still singing peace.
I look over my shoulder
   and it looks as if the whole
      world's on their
   knees, heads bowed,
    and we too are singing
    peace, and the dark
sky is snowing stars as dawn breaks.

Suddenly the world is bright
   and the Holy Child is now a Man,
    and he calls us to come
     and sit at his table.
With nail marks in his hands,
   he breaks bread and pours wine
until the whole world is fed.

We no longer are in darkness.
Stars have fallen
    into our hearts
and we sing like angels:

The miracle is Life!
Peace on earth has come!

January's Song

There is a rumor on the streets
that Christmas is over.
Lights and ornaments are packed away,
trees dragged to the curb,
people back to business as usual.
We're no longer in the party mood;
the humbugging is back in vogue.

This is January. . . .
How can Christmas be over?!
The Child is just newborn,
the song of Peace and Goodwill
still rings in our ears.
The shepherds and sages still kneel
to this One who is born to us . . .
just born to us!

How can Christmas be over??
The story of the gospel is just beginning.
We who saw the Star
now live in its Light.
We who saw and heard
now believe.

Christmas is not over.
We're just beginning
to follow this One
who calls us now to
Live in the Light of Love.
Christmas is not over.
It's just beginning
and this is January's song!!

Anything but Ordinary Time

Sticky Note the Church

On my computer there is a sticky note
with these words of Jesus:
WHO DO YOU SAY THAT I AM?
Those of us in his church
Need to sticky note the pulpit:
WHO DO YOU SAY THAT I AM?
the Pulpit
the Sanctuary
the Church School
the Session Room
the Office
the Gathering Area
the Dining Room
the Kitchen
the Elevator

Sticky note the whole church!!!!
WHO DO YOU SAY THAT I AM?

It's about Jesus

It's about Jesus. . . .
Jesus who says, Follow me.
It's about faith and following;
it's about the Truth that sets us free.
It's not about our accomplishments;
it's about his word and our faith.
It's about having the eyes to see the Way;
it's about having the ears to hear the Truth;
it's about having the hearts to live the Life,
that Life Abundant that Jesus promises.
It's about Jesus,
Jesus, the Way, the Truth, the Life.

It's about Jesus . . .
but sometimes the Church forgets.
Sometimes we in the Church
think it's about us
or the Book of Order, but
it's about Jesus. . . .
It's not about our agendas;
it's about "Follow me."
It's not about church dinners;
it's about "Feed my sheep."
It's not about forgetting
the Communion bread;
it's about remembering
that the Bread of Life
stands among us.
It's not about the
Book of Order;
it's about the love of God

written on our hearts.
It's about Jesus . . .
Jesus who calls each of us.
It's about following that call,
in spite of the difficulties,
in spite of those
who would say no.

It's about Jesus . . .
but sometimes we don't
have the eyes to see him,
or the ears to hear the
radical announcement of
peace on earth.
We don't have the hearts
to believe that
the blind can see,
the deaf can hear,
the lame can walk,
the oppressed can go free.
We don't believe there is
good news for the poor.
We've forgotten the Wonder.

Today we celebrate the persistence,
the patience, and the prayers
of these women
who did not forget the Wonder,
those who stood firm in the belief
that it was God,
and God alone,
who had called them
to preach the word
in voice or deed.

And we celebrate the women
who stood behind them and beside them
and the men who stood in solidarity
and the children
who never understood how
it could have been otherwise.

Today we celebrate because
we've come a long way,
and now we can rest and hold on
to what we have or we can keep
loving this Church forward
until every man, woman, and child
in this community of faith
has the God-given right
to seek that to which each is called.
In that day
we'll have time and energy
to be about our business
of preaching good news
and feeding his sheep.
We will remember
the astounding Wonder
and Mystery and Holiness
of our God who calls us
to love one another,
all the one anothers . . .
and the truth will set us free
to dance our faith.
And our children will never know
that it could have been otherwise.

Choices

Martha and Mary were having a party
following Sunday's evensong.
Both served on the committee
to bring the renowned pastor
for the Spring Lecture Series.
Both were also serving as liturgists.
House cleaned, specialties made,
they were prepared, as usual.

Martha, Nutritionist at St. Luke's Hospital,
and Mary, Professor of Spiritual Formation
at the Seminary, were very involved at church.
This was their favorite weekend each year.
Along with Lazarus, they had endowed the
Lecture Series in memory of their parents,
faithful and loving Christians.
Dessert and coffee afterwards had become a tradition.
Martha's specialty: devil's food and angel food cakes.
Mary's specialty: Divine Divinity and Heavenly Hash.
It was an event to savor!

An hour before the service,
Martha went to the kitchen.
Mary heard her scream and ran.
Martha stood staring at the angel food cake.
It had fallen, and Martha was distraught.
"You still have the devil's food," Mary said.
"But the guests would have no choice!
I'll have to make another cake!"

She began to take ingredients out
of the cupboard.
"There's no time now," Mary said.

"I have no choice: I have to take the time,"
Martha answered, grabbing eggs
and flour with hands that shook.
"You can read my part of the liturgy."
Mary put her hand on Martha's and
said, "Martha, do you remember
the story of Mary and Martha and
the visit of Jesus?"
"I can't believe you would bring that up!"
Martha's face was red and she frowned.
"I know you don't like it," Mary said,
"but Jesus said that Mary made the better choice
that particular time. It reminds me of this time.
Angel food cake is not important right now.
Your hospitality is always beautiful, but
because of unforeseen circumstances, we
have no angel food cake tonight or you
can put whipped cream and berries on it
or I can go to the bakery. Your choice!"
Martha threw up her hands!
"Bakery! You don't understand!
I'm *known* for this angel food cake!
You're the one known for your faith!"
Mary looked down at the floor, and
suddenly Martha burst out laughing.
Mary looked up! Tears of laughter
ran down Martha's cheeks.

Finally she said, "I suddenly had
a vision of you trying to explain
why I wouldn't be a liturgist!
She's known for her angel food cake!
How pathetic is that!"
"Let's get ready. Devil's food will do!"
Mary looked intently at her sister.
"Martha, you're known for your compassion,
your tenderheartedness, your care of the sick,
the oppressed, the scared in this world.
Don't you know, Martha?
You're known for your loving faith!"
Martha grinned: "And my angel food cake!"

Anything but Silent

Lydia owned her own business in Detroit,
a cloth dyeing business. She was partial to purple.
Her ebony skin, purple clothes, and silver jewelry
made her a knockout and she knew it.
She had been named Woman of Achievement
by the Better Business Bureau, and had several
plaques of recognition that hung on her wall.
And she was very wealthy. Not only was she
a great businesswoman, she also had inherited
from her father as well as her husband.
Her picture appeared often in society news.
Some looked at her and thought she had it all!
Lydia knew she didn't.
Saturday morning she heard a visiting evangelist
and immediately went forward for baptism,
for God had opened her heart to the words.
Her staff of women were baptized also.
Later, she offered to house the evangelist and his group,
"If you have judged me to be faithful to the Lord."
They accepted and left from her home each day to preach.
One day the evangelist had a confrontation
with a circus woman who was a fortune-teller.
She said to anyone who would listen:
"These men are servants of the Most High God!
They announce to you how you can be saved."
The evangelist thought she was mocking him, and
began telling stories of Jesus in a voice so loud
it drowned out the voice of the fortune-teller.
She heard the word of the Lord and she quit her job.
The circus threatened to sue, but the evangelist told
her not to say anything, and he would take care of it.

Now Lydia and the fortune-teller travel with the
      evangelist.
Overflowing with their new strong faith, they witness.
The fortune-teller wears a purple robe, a gift from Lydia,
and she tells the people that Jesus is in their future.
Lydia tells her own story of conversion.
She also handles the finances, giving millions away
      to the poor,
for she takes care of expenses from her own purple purse.
Lydia and the fortune-teller know the words of Jesus,
Go and preach the Gospel.
These women are anything but silent.

Light in Darkness

When I was a child, I walked in my sleep,
awaking one starless, moonless night in
the ink darkness.
Thinking I had fallen out of bed, I got up
and felt for the side of the bed,
then crawled on the floor for a while
trying to place myself in the room.
Soon I bumped into the telephone
and knew where I was . . .
across the hallway was my room,
straight across.
But to my surprise, it wasn't
across the hallway.
I went through a door,
but it was the wrong door.
It was the door to the guest room
because I felt on the wall
the cool smoothness of the fireplace tiles.
Somehow I had entered the room
next to the phone table,
not across the hall from it.
I felt confused. Nothing made sense.
And I was tired, very tired.
This time I had to be across from my room.
I exited the guest room,
and moved gingerly across the hallway.
But it was just wall that I felt on my way.
I should have come to the stairsteps down
and the stairsteps up
with its open entrance to the third floor.
Just wall, endless wall.

I walked and walked and walked,
feeling that cool wall
until finally I came to a door,
an open door.
I put my hand around the corner of the door
and felt a light switch,
but I couldn't turn on the light
as much as I wanted to!
It might be Gladys's and Daddy's room.
I can't wake them!
I decided to enter the room
and move slowly around the wall.
I heard movement and a small cry.
I was in the baby's room.
I froze and he went back into a deep sleep.
Now for sure I knew where I was!
I was across from the bathroom.
If I went to the right,
facing the wall,
I could pass the hall linen closet door.
Next would be my parents' room.
Next would be a small hallway
that would lead to the bath.
I would cross the bath,
go out the other door,
and into my room and my bed!
I was quiet, so quiet.
I walked along the wall,
and walked along the wall,
and walked along the wall,
but never ever did I get to the linen closet!
Something was terribly wrong!
I was so tired, so confused, so sleepy. . . .

I was lost!
Lost in my house!
I finally lay down on the floor.
It's got to be morning soon, I thought.
I closed my eyes,
so tired. . . .
Where on earth could I be?
I couldn't sleep as tired as I was.
I opened my eyes
and looked up.
Light!
Light from the window
on the third-floor landing.
Light!
I got up quickly,
went toward the light,
then turned swiftly to the left
into my room
into my bed,
pulling the sheets up around me.
I was saved by the Light
and the darkness had not overcome me.

Jesus Is the Door

The Earth is a globe filled with doors,
and we must choose the one to enter.
Time and again we must choose,
and our choice is daily.
Our indecision is stressful.
Our stress is great.
Which door?
Doors open, doors closed, doors ajar . . .
Doors locked, doors slammed, doors revolving . . .
Which door?
And yet . . . Jesus said I am the Door.
If we listen he will say, Follow me,
And the door will be made known.

He Is the Way, the Truth, the Life

Jesus said he was the Way, the Truth, the Life.
And he said, Follow me.
Follow me and live the Way I showed you.
Follow me and live the Truth I showed you.
Follow me and live the Life I showed you.
The Way, the Truth, the Life he showed us was Love.
Live the Way of Love.
Live the Truth of Love.
Live the Life of Love.

I heard a woman say: All we have to do is:
    Love Jesus and love one another.
Oh, yes!! all we have to do . . .

Living love is a complicated, painstaking, patient path.
An all-the-time, every time, watch-where-you're-going
way.
    Living love means making decisions all day long to
    love,
        Living love means patience with those who don't
        care about living love,
            Living love means watching our words as well
            as our actions,
                Living love means treating others as we
                ourselves want to be treated.
Living love means not hitting back,
    Living love means loving our enemies,
        Living love means loving those who speak all
        manner of evil against us.
And these things are just the beginnings of living Love.

Living Love means forgiving, means forgetting,
   Living Love means there is no room for
   self-righteousness,
      Living Love means being the people of God
      together,
a community of those who love one another
and who love all the one anothers that God created.
      Living Love means understanding those
      who hate.
Living Love means going into all the world and telling
   God's story.
He said God is Love.
He said I am the Way.
He said I am Truth.
He said I am Life.
He said Follow me.
If we have the eyes to see
And the ears to hear
Life Abundant is ours.

Jesus Is the Living Water

All you who thirst, come to the waters,
and you who have no money, come, buy, and eat!
They come . . .
Children dressed in little newly bought black suits
and dark dresses,
clutching the hands of those left to care for them.
Men and women in funereal black,
stacks of tissues in purses and pockets.
Words of ritual over the dead: Dust to dust, ashes to
ashes . . .
Oh, the ashes . . . a shroud for the mass grave that still
smolders.
They came, the wanderers, holding photos of loved ones
who never came home. . . .
They wandered, asking, pleading, wanting to believe that
at the next corner, the next phone call, the next hospital,
someone would know something.
For most of them, hope of ever seeing those loved ones,
hope of hearing those voices,
hope of holding them close is gone . . .
vanished, disappeared beneath the rubble.

They came, whispering surely not the Pentagon.
Perhaps she was out of town.
Perhaps he was out of the building,
gone to breakfast, late to work,
running an errand . . . anything.
Surely not . . .

They came, those who loved the ones
who flew on the flights of terror,

hoping against hope those they loved had missed the plane,
that there had been some mistake,
hoping, oh God, that this was the wrong flight number. . . .

They came: the firefighters who became victims,
and then more firefighters and more.
They keep on coming, and in stunning reverence,
they pray over each body they bring out.
They came: the doctors and nurses,
the police and the priests,
the construction workers,
the clean-up crews, the volunteers.

They came and will continue to come:
young soldiers going off to war,
their families saying their good-byes,
their faces full of tears and fear.

They come still in numbers too great to count:
Afghan refugees, frail and drawn,
fleeing from war they didn't make,
running for their lives,
their faces full of the horror of what they've seen,
their stomachs empty,
their children crying to them for help.

They come, the aid workers, back and forth, back and forth,
serving the ones who are serving at Ground Zero.
They come, the aid workers, trying their best to get food
and medicine to the unending line of refugees.
They come . . . the Strikes
and they continue and continue
and there is no peace.

The rest of us come giving our hearts and our spirits,
our blood and our money,
our best wishes and our prayers . . .
and our tears.
What do Christians do . . . ? What do Christians say in this
time of terror?
I saw on the back of a pickup truck these words that
someone had written following September 11th: MOURN—
CLEANUP—KILL.

The remarkable thing about that
was that we saw so little of that.
Instead the first thing our nation did was to worship.
I'd like to think the Christians,
as well as those of other faiths,
led our country to turn to God,
not out of fear, but out of conviction . . .
that through our tears,
our believing hearts know to whom they belong,
and when those hearts are nourished with the Spirit of
God,
from the believers' hearts will flow the river of living
waters.

Jesus is attending the Festival of Booths (John 7).
On the last day of the Festival is a joyous ritual
of the drawing of water,
a joyous day that harks back
to the time when the Israelites,
the whole congregation,
complained that Moses and Aaron brought them
out into the desert to die,
for they had no water,

for themselves or for their livestock.
God spoke to Moses,
telling him to gather the congregation
and to take them to the gathering place at the rock
and there Moses struck the rock with his staff
and water came out abundantly
and the congregation and their livestock drank.
Then God spoke these words to Moses and Aaron:
"'Because you did not trust in me, to show my holiness
before the eyes of the Israelites, therefore you shall not
bring this assembly into the land that I have given them.'
These are the waters of Meribah, where the people of Israel
quarreled with the LORD, and by which he showed his
holiness." (Numbers 20:12–13)

In John, Jesus said, "Let anyone who is thirsty come to me,
and let the one who believes in me drink."
And as the congregation quarreled with God in Meribah,
there was division in the crowd because of Jesus
that day at the festival during the day
of the drawing of water ritual.
The Israelites didn't have faith enough to believe
God would provide water.
Those in Jerusalem didn't have faith enough
to believe that God would provide living water.
What about the desert we're living in now?
Are people re-examining their lives?
The new house is not as important as the new heart.
The car is not as important as compassion.
An abundance of worldly goods is not as important
as the abundant life offered to us by this Jesus
who holds out his arms and says,
Come unto me all you who are thirsty.

Could it be that we are thirsting for living water?
The local, national, and international news
is filled with stories of despair.
Some stories are of generosity and love,
and who has not wept at hearing them?
Some have been stories of hatred spewed
upon anyone who even vaguely resembles
someone from the Middle East.
What are we Christians supposed to do?
The question is on our lips.
We know the answer.
We're supposed to behave like Christians.
God says to us: You know what is required: ₂
Do justice, love mercy, walk humbly with God.
Believe!!!

Believe.
Believe what?
Believe in the One who came
that you might have abundant life.
Believe in the one who said, Follow me.
Believe in the One, this Jesus, who said:
"The spirit of the Lord is upon me, because the Lord has
chosen me to bring good news to the poor, to proclaim
liberty to the captives and recovery of sight to the blind,
to set free the oppressed and announce that the time has
come when the Lord will save us."
"Let anyone who is thirsty come to me, and let the one
who believes in me drink." Out of the believers' heart
shall flow rivers of living water, for the Spirit of the Lord
will be with us.

It's all about Jesus, Jesus who says,
Come to me all you who are thirsty.
And let the one who believes in me drink.
The believers know it's about Jesus . . .
and you shall call his name Emmanuel,
God with us.
Water . . . we can't live without it.
We gather at the river
and we weep with those who weep.
Who among us does not thirst?
Soon, the humming will begin . . .
hushed and gentle and healing by the river.
And the leaves will fall. . . .
Slowly, softly, the humming will turn to song,
a new song that comes from believing hearts,
and the snows will come . . .
and through it all, the arms of God are open to us.
"Sir, give me this living water that I might never
thirst again."
Out of the believers' heart shall flow rivers of living water.
Jesus is the Living Water.

There Is But One Whose Name Is Peace

There is but One
whose name is Peace
One whose heart is peace—
       whose soul is peace—
       whose mind is peace.
And the world knew him not.

And so they killed him
because they didn't want
to share their bread
       and their wine.

Today the world is covered in blood,
but still the Prince of Peace
calls to us: Follow me.

There is but One
whose name is Peace.
Those who believe
       in the midst of violence
       in the midst of torture
       in the midst of war war war
have no choice
but to shout from the rooftops:
Peace on earth!!

I believe in peace on earth!

Peace, Peace

The world has become the valley of the shadow of death,
but we who believe are asked to walk it without fear,
asked to remember that our Shepherd will not leave us.
We're up to our hearts in the daily death count,
blood spurting at us from our televisions
and leaving our hands smeared
when we read the morning paper.
All over the world the children of God
are killing one another,
and the bands play and the
flag-draped bodies come home,
and God is invoked to bless it all.
Peace, Peace, but there is no peace. . . .
The killing and the maiming continue.

The world sits in the Chair of Despair,
dismissing those who preach peace.
"Dreamers!" they shout,
and somehow "dreamers"
sounds like a curse word,
as the word "Peace"
sounds unpatriotic while
the word "War" sounds
strong and mighty . . .
righteous and just,
and godly.

There is no sanctuary
for those who preach peace,
for patriotism trumps faith,
and besides, the church is busy
with its own quarreling.

Too busy for peace . . .
too busy for peace . . .
There is no sanctuary
for those who seek peace
except in the word of God,
except in the heart of God.
In the word of God
we find the Prince of Peace
who today walks through the blood
and picks his sheep up in his arms,
one by one,
and takes them home.
Then he runs and strides into
our church sanctuaries,
right down the carpeted aisles,
ignoring the blood on his sandals,
and stands before the church
and says, "Follow me."
We'll be there soon, we answer,
just as soon as we finish our quarreling.
"Love one another," says
the Prince of Peace,
those bloody sandals trying
to walk into our hearts.
But the church is terribly busy
with its own quarreling.
No, there is no sanctuary
for those who preach peace.

Peace, peace, there is no peace.
The world shakes its head
at protest and prayer.
"Dreamers!"

They scream again,
but those who preach peace
know that peace is not a dream.
Those who preach peace know
in their hearts that they do not
have to apologize in the
Church of Jesus Christ
for the words of the Prince of Peace.
Peace is a promise, a promise
from the heart of God
to our hearts.
Go in the promise of that peace.
Go knowing that this church and this world
belong to the Prince of Peace
no matter what,
no matter what.

No matter what, feed his sheep.
No matter what, love one another.
No matter what, preach peace
in the assembly of the world
and in the assembly of the church.
No matter what, believe that
Peace will come,
for peace is not a dream.
Peace is a promise.

Go now to tell the others.
Go now to shout it from the rooftops.
Shout it in the name of Jesus,
Jesus, the Prince of Peace. Amen.

Everyone Wants Peace

The man on the platform called for peace, and the crowd cheered him. He felt good deep down inside: the people want peace.

He went to the soldiers on the battlefield and cried, the people want peace. So do we, said the soldiers, but we must take our orders from the generals.

So he went to the generals and said, the people and the soldiers want peace. So do we, said the generals, but we must take our orders from the politicians.

So he went to the politicians and said, the people and the soldiers and the generals want peace. So do we, said the politicians, but the enemy won't stop their warring.

So he went to the enemy and said, our side wants peace, the people and the soldiers and the generals and the politicians. So do we, said the enemy, but the diplomats won't arrange it.

So he went to the diplomats and said, Everyone wants peace, the people, the soldiers, the generals, the politicians, and the enemy. Why can't you arrange it?

What is peace? asked the diplomats. There is no peace: there is only peace if . . .
The people want peace if they can have more land and better life.

The soldiers want peace if they can go home and be paid a big pension. The generals want peace if they can have more power.
The politicians want peace if they can get re-elected.
The enemy wants peace if they can have everything better than ever . . . for themselves.
There is no peace, said the diplomats.

The man on the platform cried out at the people. You don't want peace, he said. You and the soldiers and the generals and the politicians and the enemy. Even the diplomats no longer believe in their mission of peace. You say peace, but what you want is something for yourselves.

No, No! cried people. What we want is for our children. All this . . . all this war and sacrifice, this bloodshed and terror . . . all this so our children can have a good life.

The man on the platform cried for peace . . . costly Peace . . . and the people turned away calling him a fanatic.

Prayer for Peace Seekers

Lean close, O Holy God!
Lean close and hear the weeping hearts of your people
    who seek peace!

The map of your world is dark with death!
Your earth is saturated with the blood of your children!
The innocents cry for help, and are answered with silence.
War and terror stalk us! Fear is at every doorstep.
O God, your people are killing one another . . .
and sometimes in your name!
We who seek peace raise our voices to sing
and are drowned out by explosive obscenities of hatred.
We walk the path of peace and are stopped by a world on
    fire with war.
We are taunted by sounds of derision . . .
and sometimes in your name!
O God, bless the peace seekers!
O God, give us your hand!

Give us patience, O God, when our faith falters.
Give us stamina to stand up and walk in your peace!
Give us tenderheartedness for those who think War is
    the answer.
Give the world the eyes to see the absurdity of killing!
Soften the hearts of all nations, O Holy One,
and have mercy upon us all!
Come, O Holy God, come, and save your world!

Pull your Church into its pulpits to preach your
       Word of Peace!
Pull your People onto rooftops to sing their Song
       of Peace!
Give us new voices, O God!
Give us new songs!
Give us new hearts for one another, for all the one
       anothers!!
Give us new Hope!
Give us new Life!
O God, send Angels!
Send Miracles!
Send Love!
Send Peace!

In the name of Jesus
whose birth was surrounded by the Angels' song of
       Peace, Goodwill,
whose life was a covenant of Peace and Love,
whose death and resurrection were the ultimate word of
       your Grace!
We give you thanks, O God, for your never-ending gift of
       Life! Amen.

I No Longer Pray for Peace

On the edge of war, one foot already in,
I no longer pray for peace:
I pray for miracles.

I pray that stone hearts will turn
to tenderheartedness,
and evil intentions will turn
to mercifulness,
and all the soldiers already deployed
will be snatched out of harm's way,
and all the frightened innocents
will be saved from the obscenities of war,
and the whole world will be
astounded onto its knees.

I pray that all the "God talk" will take bones,
and stand up and shed its cloak of faithlessness,
and walk again in its powerful truth.
I pray that the whole world might
sit down together and share
its bread and its wine.
Some say there is no hope,
but then I've always
applauded the holy fools
who never seem to give up on
the scandalousness of our faith:
that we are loved by God . . .
that we can truly love one another.

I no longer pray for peace.
I pray for miracles.

No2Torture!

What happened that the world doesn't know
what the church stands for?
What happened? What happened? What happened?

What have we in the church been doing
when we should have been voicing,
should have been making clear
who we are . . .
who Jesus is????

Has it come to this?
That we in the church must say,
must shout,
must stand
for what we believe?
Does the world no longer know us
by our fruits?

Do we have to have a discussion
to inform the world that the Church says
No2Torture?

Is there any doubt that
The Church of Jesus Christ
does not condone torture?
Any question,
any room for discussion?

What happened to
The Church of Jesus Christ?
Jesus who said,

"Love your neighbor as you love yourself"?
Jesus who said,
"Do unto others as you would have
them do unto you"?
What happened?
Who is it who came along and
changed the Word of God?
There is no room for
torture in the words of Jesus.
He did not say:
Return evil for evil.
He did not say:
Hit back.
He said, Turn the other cheek.
He said, Love your enemies.
He said, Follow me.

The world should have heard us
shouting good news from the rooftops,
singing Alleluias in the streets of the world!
The world should have seen us
praying for our enemies.
The world should have seen us
following the Prince of Peace.

Oh, God, may they see us now!

Oh, God, may they hear us now!

No2Torture!!!!

My Mother's Bible

In the beginning was the Word, and the Word was with
God, and the Word was God. . . . All things came into
being through him, and without him not one thing came
into being. What has come into being in him was life, and
the life was the light of all people. The light shines in the
darkness, and the darkness has not overcome it.

My mother's Bible sits on my bookshelf.
When I open it, I see her
handwriting in the margins,
often with the dates of the readings
or her thoughts or her hopes or her grief.
This day there was no date.
The Scripture was Matthew 5,
The Beatitudes, of course,
and these verses are marked:
verse 9: "Blessed are the peacemakers,
for they will be called children of God."
verse 11: "Blessed are you when people
revile you and persecute you and utter
all kinds of evil against you falsely
on my account."
In the margin is the word "Tom,"
my father.
Persecuted for righteousness' sake.
She would say that quite often
during those days.
My father . . .
persecuted for righteousness' sake.
How? I asked.
Your father's going to have

to leave this church
because he preached something
people didn't like to hear.
It's about Peace, she said.
Who would have thought
a sermon on peace would
have everybody in church
so riled up?
They told your father
to stick to the Bible.
She laughed.
I thought peace was in the Bible, I said.
So did I, my mother said. So did I.
And she left for the kitchen laughing.
Stick to the Bible indeed!

I was not quite seven when
my father preached peace.
My theology amounted to
"God is love," "Be ye kind,"
and "Love one another."
They were repeated constantly
around our house,
usually by my brother
who wanted me to
do something for him.
My mother said those verses
were all about peace.
Jesus himself preached peace.
My brother and I knew
that the people at church
were mad at our father,
but we didn't understand

why it was about this sermon.
If Jesus wants peace
and Daddy wants peace,
what's so bad about it?
Jesus wants peace,
my mother said,
and Daddy wants peace,
but there are church people
who don't want peace.
That was hard for me to believe.
Who wouldn't want peace?
Who in the world wouldn't want peace?
Who in the church wouldn't want peace?

I think of that conversation then
and many others like it and how
that sermon changed our lives,
but for the life of me,
I still don't understand
why a Christian pastor
would hesitate to preach peace
in the Church of Jesus Christ,
then or now.

There was going to be a war
whether Jesus and my father
liked it or not, and
my mother was more
worried than ever.
Every time some committee met,
we would find our mother with Kleenex
and she would say how her eyes watered
when she sliced onions.

There on the cutting board would be
an onion at least half-sliced.
It was an amazing coincidence.

The Session met and said
my father should not resign although
he had offered his resignation.
A vote of the congregation
was overwhelmingly supportive
of my father, but there were a few
elders who requested that the matter
be brought before Presbytery.
The Presbytery committee on ministry
met and reported that our father was
a man of faith, but because of
the nature of the quarrel,
he should resign so there
would be no divisiveness
in the church.
Since the Presbytery committee
had no authority to dissolve
the ministerial covenant,
my father appealed to Synod.
Synod met and praised my father
for his Christian faith and ministry.
They said he was following
his conscience and was a faithful
servant of Jesus Christ.
My father returned to the Session
and resigned, saying
that he could only preach
from a free pulpit.
Our father had been tried

for heresy in the Presbyterian Church
and had been acquitted,
but now he had no pulpit at all.
We would, however, stay
while my father got things in order.

My mother said she was going
to the Women's Association
and that she would stand up
for what she believed, too.
I felt sad that my mother
had been hurt so terribly.
When my mother cried,
I felt like crying, too.
Why would people
in the church
hurt my mother?
Off we went to the Women's Association.
We went every Tuesday.
I loved it because they served
cheese dreams, toasted cheese
sandwiches browned in lots of butter.
On that Tuesday it seemed quiet
when we went in, but soon one
of the ladies called my name,
and another got up and came to my mother,
and took her hand,
and pretty soon we were all eating
cheese dreams and laughing.
It was my mother who
taught the Bible study
that day.
Later she told my father

that she had talked about
the Beatitudes and how
my father had let his light
shine before others so that
they could see his good works
and give glory to God.
My father said that sounded
a little grand to him,
that it just came down to
preaching the gospel or not.
I'm proud of you,
my mother said to him,
very proud.
You've stood up and
you've been counted.
I'm very proud of you, too,
my father said.
I know all this is hard on you.
And then he told her
that people at the church
had not remembered
to "Be ye kind."
They were calling our Daddy
names . . . bad names.
What was even more surprising
was that they were calling
my mother names, too.
Don't pay any attention,
our mother would say to us:
We're standing up for Jesus.
Jesus says love one another,
all the one anothers . . .
and she would tell us

the stories of Jesus,
and she was right.
It all came down to loving each other;
it all came down to covenant keeping.
It was about living the faith.

How can your father minister
to the congregation if he doesn't
take a stand on the things that really
matter in life?
How can he say that Jesus wants war?
How can he say Jesus wants
the people working in Nashville
to have these low wages?
How can he say Jesus
doesn't love Norvella
just because her skin is black?
It's those three things,
my mother said,
Jesus is the one who said them.
Your father preached
what Jesus said.
It's all right, I said,
Daddy told the truth.
Her eyes began to well up,
and I was afraid she'd go
hunting for some onions,
but she just hugged me.
I know, she whispered.
Did you know that Truth
is another name for Jesus?
I shook my head. I didn't.
My mother knew so many things!

Jesus Is the Bread of Life
Mark 8:14–21

(Speaker throws baskets one by one onto the floor.)

one two three four five six seven eight nine ten eleven twelve
and
one two three four five six seven

Do you not yet understand?
They forgot the bread.
Forgot to stop on the way
for a few loaves of bread.
It was one of those details
that fell through the cracks.
Of course, they had been busy . . .
busy with crowd control,
busy feeding five thousand,
busy feeding four thousand,
busy cleaning up,
putting away the leftovers
into twelve baskets,
into seven baskets.
It wasn't that they were
irresponsible.
When you're in charge
of General Assembly,
you're allowed a few glitches.
But still . . . they had no bread.
It was then he spoke:
"Watch out for
the leaven of the Pharisees
and the leaven of Herod."

Being the resourceful leaders they were,
they huddled in committee,
one by one speaking
about the bread problem,
wondering if they should bring in
an expert on conflict resolution.
He heard their discussion
and said: Why are you
talking about bread?
Do you not yet understand?
Are your hearts still hardened?

Understand?
Hadn't Jesus himself mentioned
the leaven of the Pharisees,
the leaven of Herod?
Wasn't Jesus talking about bread?
Leaven could mean bread,
but it could also mean teachings.
Was Jesus telling them to
beware of the teachings of the Pharisees?
Beware of the infectious anxiety
about rules and regulations,
the seductive busyness concerning
traditions and appearances.
Beware of the subtle yeast
that bubbles up,
giving ritual priority
over spirituality.
Beware of the temptation
of self-righteousness.
Beware of being woven
together in hypocrisy.

Beware of mistaking church work
for discipleship.
Beware of hardened hearts.
The disciples recognized
the false teachings
of the Pharisees,
but Jesus was not talking
to the Pharisees;
he was talking to the disciples.
Do you not yet understand?

And what about the Herodians?
They weren't teachers;
their leaven was worldliness.
Beware of the secular world.
Beware of the subtle ways
in which Caesar demands our allegiance.
Beware of bowing down to false gods.
Beware of compromising your faith.
Beware of the power of possessions
and the possessiveness of power.
The disciples knew of the evil way
of those who worked for Herod,
but Jesus wasn't talking
to the Herodians.
Jesus was talking to the disciples.
He was talking to the ones
he had chosen to follow him.
He was talking to the ones chosen
to go into all the world
and tell the good news.

It is to the disciples
that Jesus said:
Are your hearts hardened?

Jesus spoke again:
You have eyes;
don't you see?
After all we've been through together,
don't you have the eyes to see?
You have ears,
can't you hear?
After all I've taught you,
don't you have the ears to hear?

And don't you remember?
Jesus reminds them with questions:
"When I broke the five loaves of bread
for the five thousand,
how many baskets full
of broken pieces of bread
were left over?"
The disciples answered: Twelve.
"And when I broke the seven loaves
for the four thousand,
how many baskets full
of broken pieces
did you pick up?"
They answered: Seven.
"Do you not yet understand?"

Why are you anxious about
what we're going to have
for supper tonight
when you have just seen me
multiply bread
to feed the hungry.
You have eyes;
can't you see?
And why are you worried
that you forgot the bread
when you have heard
me quote the scriptures:

> One does not live by bread alone,
> but by every word that comes
> from the mouth of the LORD. (Deut. 8:3)

You have ears,
why can't you hear?

Don't you remember?
Don't you yet understand?
You are stressed
and anxious
because you forgot
the bread
when the Bread of Life
stands among you.
Twelve and seven baskets
full of pieces of bread . . .
Don't you yet understand?

Lo and Behold

Once upon a time,
In the land of Lo and Behold,
That land of miracles and mysteries,
That land of wonder after wonder,
That land where the Creator walked the earth,
And said, "Ah, this is good,"
That land where almost from the beginning
The creatures deceived the Creator and
Blamed it on a neighborhood snake,
That land where God's creatures traded a garden
For murder and mayhem,
Right there in the land of Lo and Behold,
Which God decided to destroy
To put an end to the evil,
And would have, too,
If it hadn't been for
Righteous and faithful Noah,
Who built an ark and
Set out in and survived the flood
With a family and a zoo
In the land of Lo and Behold,
That land where God made a covenant
And a promise that whenever
A rainbow appeared in the sky,
God would remember
The covenant with the people
In the land of Lo and Behold,
That land where a man wrestled with God,
And where a boy in a rainbow robe,
A boy who interpreted dreams,
A boy who was thrown into a pit by his jealous brothers

And left for dead, became a ruler in Egypt.
Second only to Pharaoh,
That land where old Sarah
Gave birth to a much wanted child,
In the land of Lo and Behold,
That land in which God
Promised that Sarah and Abraham
Would have more descendants
Than all the stars in the skies
In the land of Lo and Behold,
That land in which a Hebrew child
Grew up in Pharaoh's palace,
And was called by God to lead
All the people out of slavery,
And, in spite of the magic tricks
And the plagues and crossing the Red Sea,
The Hebrews escaped and
God sent bread from heaven
And water from a rock,
And laws to live by,
But still the people wanted to worship idols,
In the land of Lo and Behold,
That land where a prostitute named Rahab
Hid the Israelite spies and saved her family
With a crimson cord,
That land where Joshua
With trumpets and shouts
Brought down the walls of Jericho
In the land of Lo and Behold,
That land where Samuel, the prophet of God,
Anointed a shepherd boy to become king,
That land where this shepherd boy
Took his slingshot and killed a giant,

And became a mighty warrior,
But best of all, became a poet!
In the land of Lo and Behold,
That land where there were many kings,
Some good, some bad,
That land where God's prophets
Announced God's will to the kings and to the people,
That land where most of the kings and the people
Turned their backs on the prophets and on God,
That land where the people still
Wanted to worship idols,
In the land of Lo and Behold,
It came to pass that
A child was born to us,
Born not in the house of kings and queens,
But in the house of animals
Where his mother nursed him,
And his father walked him,
And angels appeared
In the loudest Lo and Behold of all,
And shepherds came to worship him,
And sages came to bring gifts,
And the angels sang Peace into the dark night
In that little town of Bethlehem,
Bombed and battled and bullet-infested Bethlehem,
Where the angels still sing, PEACE,
Where God's people have forgotten the words,
In the land of Lo and Behold,
Where almost from the beginning
The child's life was in danger,
The murder and mayhem unerased
From the souls of God's people,
In this land of Lo and Behold,

Where God sent an angel to Lo and Behold
To Joseph, and the family fled
Into Egypt, and were saved,
And Jesus grew and was baptized,
And was tempted by Satan, and
Attended to by angels, and he
Preached to the people to repent,
For the people still wanted to worship idols,
In the land of Lo and Behold,
Where Jesus healed the sick,
Even on the Sabbath,
And ate with tax collectors
And befriended prostitutes
And outcasts and children,
And cleansed lepers and stilled a storm,
And he told the people to love one another
As much as they wanted to be loved,
And not to judge each other, and not to worry,
And not to store up treasures on earth,
But to give from the heart,

And Jesus told them: Feed my sheep,
And he was grieved at their hardness of heart
In the land of Lo and Behold,
Where Jesus told the people parables
So they could better understand the word of God,
And, even though they gave him a parade into Jerusalem,
And he had an intimate supper with his closest friends,
He was betrayed, and deserted,
Deserted not only by the crowds who
Had only a few days ago shouted Hosanna,
But also by his disciples who left him all alone,
And Peter, on whom Jesus was to build his Church,

Said to the servant girl, "I do not know this man,"
And Jesus was crucified and resurrected,
Ascended to heaven,
But he did not leave the people helpless,
But left for them the Holy Spirit,
Who is here and ready to give life
In the land of Lo and Behold,
Where we are killing each other
In the name of the Lord,
Blood spilling, not only in the streets of Jerusalem,
Not only in the little town of Bethlehem,
But all over the world,
And within the Church we deny who he is,
And we say we do not know this man,
For we do not have the ears to hear God's story,
For we still want to worship idols,
Idols within the church of power and greed and rightness,
And we do not listen to the prophets or to God,
For we live in our own little kingdoms
Where we spend our time furthering our careers,
For we have made idols of our own opinions,
And we love to hear the sound of our own voices
In the land of Lo and Behold,
Where we no longer pay attention
To the miracles and the mystery,
Or to the wonder upon wonder
In the land of Lo and Behold,
For we've forgotten the promises and possibilities
Of faithfulness,
We've forgotten the dreams and the passion of our
mission
In the land of Lo and Behold
Where God walks the earth

Calling us to be about the holy business of God,
Calling us to look at one another in tenderheartedness,
Calling us to stop our quarreling and work together
To feed God's sheep,
Calling us to mercy for those who
Hunger for the Bread of Life,
Calling us to humbly live in community
Working together, not for our own sakes,
But for Jesus' sake in the land of Lo and Behold,
Where, Lo and Behold, even now we can hear
The voice of God calling: Return to Me,
Even now, Return to Me.

Lent

We All Have Our Courtyards

We all have our courtyards,
those times and places we face
like Peter
when we must decide
to stand up and say
whether we know him or not.
Those crossroads in our lives,
when we go along with things as they are,
or we say, as Luther did,
Here I stand, I can do no other.
We all have our courtyards. . . .
Lent is the time to prepare
for our courtyards,
the time to listen to who *he* says he is.
And he did, you know,
He did tell us who he is.
He is that one who brings good news to the poor,
freedom to the oppressed,
sight to the blind . . .
that Holy One who said,
Follow me.
Feed my sheep.

Jesus, God's Beloved Son
Mark 1:9–15

When I was a child we didn't have Lent,
not down in Nashville, Tennessee,
where my father was a Presbyterian minister.
That's not to say there wasn't any of that "giving up"
        business going on;
It's just that Presbyterians didn't do it.
Oh, we waved our fronds as we went into the sanctuary
        on Palm Sunday,
and we observed Holy Week,
the most memorable day being Friday
when we had hot cross buns and didn't go to school,
but went instead to the worship service downtown,
and listened to one of those Last Words Sermons
and afterwards ate at the B & W cafeteria.
I was afraid a truant officer would see us,
but my mother assured me she'd never seen a
        truant officer
lurking around in the churches in Nashville, Tennessee.
What we did see was a lot of people going to church on
        Good Friday
and a lot of people praying.
I knew something very important was going on,
and that it was about Jesus.
Not Easter baskets, not new clothes, not Easter dinner.
        Jesus.
It was about Jesus.

It was also about Jesus when my father was tried by the
    church for heresy.
He had preached sermons about racial equality
    and higher wages for the poor
    and loving people of other faiths,
as well as preaching a sermon on peace just before
    World War II.
Some people told him to stick to the Bible.
My father said he was preaching the gospel,
and his conscience would only allow him
to preach the truth as he saw it.
As he heard it.
As he felt the Spirit.
It was about Jesus.

Many Lents later, I have taped to my desk these words:
Who do you say that I am?
They are Jesus' words to the disciples.
They are Jesus' words to me every time I sit down
    to write.
Who do *you* say that I am?

And I anguish.
We all think we know, and yet, we're a church quarreling
because we don't agree who Jesus is.

When Jesus appeared by the Jordan,
John knew who Jesus was,
and baptized him.

God, of course, identified him in front of the crowd:
"You are my beloved Son."

In our congregation the baptized are given small
        needlepoint rainbows
as reminders of God's covenant with Noah and with us.
They are then welcomed into the family of faith.

In the wilderness, Satan knew who Jesus was
and tempted him when he was famished,
as we are tempted when we are famished,
whether it be for food
or shelter
or recognition
or wealth
or power
or love.

Jesus went to Galilee preaching the gospel,
saying, "The time is fulfilled, and the kingdom of God has
        come near;
    repent, and believe in the good news."
But the good news was not always received as such . . .
not then, not now.

The trouble was the good news proved
too scandalous, too radical, too good to be true,
and they turned their backs on Jesus . . .
the people, the religious authorities, the government,
and even the disciples,
and Jesus suffered unto death . . . alone.
As the spiritual says, "We didn't know who you [were]."
My prayer is that this Lent we will know who he is,
and we will "give up" our hearts to a world
who screams for a word of hope from the Church of
        Jesus Christ.

I pray we will have the ears to hear the good news
and the courage to preach it,
the eyes to see who Jesus is and the love to follow:
Feeding his sheep,
living in peace with one another, all the one anothers,
standing up and taking risks for his word,
and believing that God's arms are open to us
    in mercy
    and forgiveness
    and unfailing Love
in this powerful gift
of covenant faithfulness.

Peter Had Called Him Messiah
Mark 8:31–38

Through the Lenten window
the loudspeaker blares "Repent and Believe."
We light our candle and try to see through the darkness.
The loudspeaker won't stop:
Repent and believe. Repent and believe. Repent and
      believe.
On and on and on and on.

In the distance through the noise
Jesus is speaking.
Suffer. Rejection. Death. Rise in three days.
Peter's voice now through the loudspeaker,
over the voice of Jesus.
"God forbid it, Lord. This must never happen to you."
Then the One who had earlier called Peter the Rock
on whom he would build his Church,
now calls Peter Satan! Get behind me, Satan!
Peter, a stumbling block, worldly, not godly.
Peter who had followed Jesus immediately,
      fiercely, faithfully,
Peter who knew Jesus, Peter who called Jesus
      the Messiah,
This Peter was now a stumbling block to the One whom
      he so fervently loved!
Repent and believe! Repent and believe!
Through the Lenten window we cry out:
We love you fervently, too!
But our voices make no noise.
All we hear is Repent and believe!
Jesus has called Peter Satan.

Our eyes look down the road to that day in the courtyard
of Caiaphas
when once more Peter will say: I do not know him.
What is it we will say when these forty days are gone?
What will we say in that courtyard?
The loudspeaker stops.
Jesus is speaking:
Who do you say that I am?

Our eyes look down, wishing we weren't here,
yet he speaks to us in the crowd,
his eyes compelling us to look and to listen:
If you want to follow me,
lose your lives in feeding my sheep.
But we do we do we do we do.
We do feed your sheep.
We in the church are good about feeding sheep.
All you have to do, Jesus, is to look at the church budget
to see how many sheep have been fed.
Funny it was Peter who said to the crowd
to hell with your money.
Later, of course, Peter was preaching,
preaching the good news,
the good news that God is with us.
Why is it so hard for us to believe that?
The earth is filled with the tears of God, for all over
the world
the children of God are hating,
hurting,
killing each other.
The suffering is immense, unbearable,
but the Church cannot find its voice.

The blood of the dead splats against our faces;
the maimed scream into our hearts;
we cover our eyes and listen
but our ears hear the droning of the death count rising.
How awful, we whisper,
then turn back to our quarreling.
You would think we could weep.
When my father felt there was no longer a free pulpit
from which he could speak, he resigned.
He said that the greatest temptation came
from well-meaning good friends
who begged him to compromise.
I believe in compromise, he said,
but the gospel cannot be compromised.

Oh, Peter, the gospel can't be compromised.
Oh, Church, the gospel cannot be compromised!

Follow me and you will see me suffer.
His eyes bore into our souls. You will also suffer for
        my sake.
By the world's standards you may not be successful,
but the word of God is not about worldly success;
it's about Jesus and covenant faithfulness.

The earth is filled with the tears of God,
but the earth is also filled with the people of God,
as many as all the stars in the sky.
It was the covenant promise to Abraham and Sarah
and they believed . . . descendants more than all the stars
        in the sky.
They believed. They believed

With all those stars in our covenant sky,

surely the voice of the Church of the Prince of Peace
    will be heard.

Surely!

Through our Lenten window we begin to see Light.

He looks at us, those eyes piercing into our souls.

Follow me, he says.

Diluting the Gospel
John 2:13–22

Our church school teacher tried to dilute the story,
but I had a picture of Jesus with the whip in his hand
The whip was snapping . . . I could almost hear it . . .
The moneychangers cowered against the whip's threat;
Tables were overturned.
Some of the men were up and running.
The cows and sheep were scattering.
Doves were scrambling in their cages.
Coins were rolling and flying through the air.
The face of Jesus showed fury!
Cows and sheep and doves sold for sacrifices,
Roman money changed into the Tyrian shekels
required for the annual head tax
that went into the temple treasury.
In other words, it was church business.
But Jesus thought otherwise:
God's house was being desecrated.
He drove the moneychangers out of the temple.

But that was then
and that was that.
Except of course,
they did tear down the temple . . .
Jesus' temple
and he did rebuild it three days later.
Crucifixion. Resurrection.
Then the disciples understood
that the Church was the Body of Jesus.

O Jesus, you showed us God
when you showed yourself,
but we didn't see, we didn't see.
The Word of God walked across our lives,
but we didn't hear, we didn't hear.
We didn't allow your footsteps
to crunch into our souls.
We stuck to business as usual,
even church business,
even on Sunday.
And our tables are up for overturning.

Give us a sign
Give us a sign

And we who have the rainbow
and all the stars in the sky
ask God for further ID.
As though there were no ten commandments,
as though we were never told
that God will not stand for idolatry.
As though we never heard of being
the people of God.
As though we never heard
of living with God in covenant.
There will be no other gods before me.
No other gods.
As though Jesus never said
You shall love the Lord your God
with all your heart, and soul and mind,
and you shall love your neighbor as yourself
as yourself as yourself.
I am the Way and the Truth and the Life.

Come, follow me.
Come, walk with me.
Come, Life Abundant is with me.

"The heavens declare the glory of God!"
and yet, we forget to look out our windows
and we miss the word of God
from Day to Day!
"God's law is perfect!
More to be desired than gold
even much fine gold."
The coins for which we give our souls
are worthless compared to Life Abundant!

I showed my father the picture
of Jesus with the whip in his hand
and asked why Jesus was so mad
at the people in the temple.
Because, he said, they didn't believe.
They didn't walk in covenant with God.
They had no reverence for God's word.
I'm glad, I said, that we believe.
My father let me walk away in innocence.
No other gods, and yet this Lent
we stumble over the gods in our sanctuaries,
stubbing our toes on gods of Self-Importance,
    Self-Righteousness, and Egotism.
We bow down to Wealth and War and Power and Status
    and Possessions and
Rules and Divisiveness as well as Our Own Agendas.

The list goes on and on
add to it or subtract,
it makes no difference.

The gods are there
waiting to be fed.
Even the pastor can become an idol.
Even Jesus when we make him
in our own image.
Who do we say that he is?
And how can we live
with what we've been saying??

Jesus couldn't live with the mockery
of the moneychangers in the temple.
His faith was fierce.
There was no compromising.
He lived and died so that we could live . . .
abundantly
with God
in covenant
in community
in faith.

Forgive, O God, our mockery.
Forgive our agenda keeping
rather than covenant keeping.
Forgive the arrogance of preferring
our own words to yours.
Forgive our egotism
that leads us to think
we are wiser than you.

Forgive our busyness that makes
us turn away from this war-pocked world.
Forgive us our divisiveness
that they might say of us again:
"How those Christians love one another!"
Forgive our controlling ways,
our bowing down to power and wealth and greed.
Forgive us for making rules
we'd rather follow than yours.
Give us the eyes to see Jesus
the courage to stand up
and speak out in his name
the love to feed the hungry
the compassion to heal the sick
the faithfulness to love mercy
the covenant stamina
to do justice in your name
and, O God, the humility
to walk in covenant with you.
During this Lenten time
give us the hearts to hear your word
and give us, we pray,
the only Bread and Wine we need.

God So Loved the World
John 3:14–21

I've never been bitten by a serpent
although one early dawn hour
I was awakened by my brother
who appeared quite happy
since he had just recovered his lost snake
under my bed.
Perhaps I, unlike the poor Israelites,
was spared because I don't ever remember
complaining about my mother's cooking,
but complain about the food the Israelites did.
Even though God had sent water and manna
and an occasional quail,
the Israelites said they detested the miserable food.
God, who had saved them *from* captivity
and was saving them *for* the Promised Land,
had had it with their complaining,
to say nothing of their unfaithfulness,
so sent serpents who bit their ankles
and many Israelites died.
In great fear the Israelites ran to Moses
to pray that God would forgive them
and rid them of the serpents.
Moses built a poisonous serpent of bronze,
as God had instructed,
and set it high on a pole.
The ones who were bitten
were to look at "the brazen serpent"
and be saved.

The belief in God's saving power—
not any magic of the serpent—
brought life.
Jesus thought the serpent story important enough
to tell to the people in his day,
explaining that just as Moses lifted up
the serpent in the wilderness,
the Son of Man would be lifted up
so that the believers could keep their eyes on him
and be saved for eternal life.
Of course, Jesus would be lifted up on a cross,
and Jesus would die for their sins . . . and ours.
"O give thanks to the Lord for God is good
God's steadfast love endures forever."
We taught it to our children.
Too bad the Israelites didn't give thanks
instead of complaining.
Moses had told them to trust in God.
Believe and you'll go to the Promised Land,
but I guess it sounded just too good to be true.
Just as grace sounded to the people in Jesus' day.
Just as grace sounds to us today.
    For God so loved the world . . .
The melody of the anthem
we sang in the church choir
when I was in high school
floats over me,
embeds itself in me,
repeats itself . . .
    that God gave his only begotten Son . . .
The days of Lent are passing too quickly.
Almost over almost over.
Where have the days gone?

What have we done?
that whoso believeth, believeth in him . . .
Keep your eyes on me.
Shall not perish shall not perish
Eyes on me.
but have everlasting life
everlasting life
Eyes on me.

Many did, many didn't
keep their eyes on Jesus.
Many do, many don't
keep their eyes on Jesus.

God gave covenant
commandments
laws
life
freedom
promise
hope
and love . . .
and they complained
about the food.
The story makes me nervous.

For God so loved the world
that God gavegavegavegave
gave his only Son
that whoever believes in him
will have everlasting life.
Gave!
We don't have to earn it.

If we believe we will follow we will live.
Believe follow live.
Live because you follow because you believe
God's good news.

We met Jesus in the hall
and he asked where we'd been.
In the plenary, we answered.
Why? he asked.
We thought that's where
you wanted us to be, we said.
Why? he asked.
Because, we answered,
that's where the decisions are made.
He looked at us and said:
The decisions have already been made.
We looked at each other,
not knowing what to say.
Who do you say that I am? he asked.
Luckily for us, Peter had already
answered this one.
The Messiah, we said in chorus,
hoping we'd get applause
just as Peter did.
Without a word he said,
Keep your eyes on me,
and started down the hall.
We followed although the crowd
became thick and he walked quickly.
Every once in a while, he would turn,
Keep your eyes on me.
We asked him to tell us
where he was going

in case we got lost.
If you keep your eyes on me,
you won't be lost.
But where, we cried,
are we going???
Into the world, he said.
    not into the world
        to condemn the world
The melody again . . .
    but to save the world.
Into the world, he said,
into the world.
Come, follow.
We were tired trying to
keep our eyes on Jesus
and walk through the crowded streets
all at the same time.
Don't you understand? we asked,
we are your church.
We go into all the world all the time;
we've done so many things
in your name.
Don't you know how much we do?
Suddenly we stand in the Lenten darkness,
hearing our own complaining voices,
snakes slithering around our ankles
under our beds.
We cry out, for Jesus has disappeared.
Neon lights flash words into the dark:

    You congratulate yourselves
    on your good works
    and yet, you yourselves were saved.

and not by your own doing,
but God's,
so that no one can boast.
By grace you have been saved through faith.

And then silence.

Just when we think we know you,
just when we're sure who you are
and where it is you're sending us
and to what it is you're calling us,
just when we're comfortable in the pew,
just then is when
you move out of your frame
and do something new
and entirely unexpected.
O Expected One,
you are never the one we expect.

You said, Follow me;
we looked away for just a moment
and you disappeared down a street
and we stand in darkness
lost without you.
Have mercy on us, for we meant to
keep our eyes on you,
but we were afraid we'd have to follow you
into the midst of war or torture or poverty.
We're afraid we'd have to hold a dying world in our arms.
We confess our trivial worlds loom larger
    than your word.
We confess we keep our eyes on our own wants and fears
    instead of on you.

We confess we make excuses
for not following you into
broken hearts
broken lives
broken bodies
broken bonds
broken promises
broken homes
broken communities
broken nations
this broken world
O God, we confess the brokenness of your Church.
Give us life once more in the light of your Word!

In the silence of our prayer we wait for his forgiveness.
Light comes and once more he's saying:
Keep your eyes on me and you will live!

We Would See Jesus
John 12:20–33

Broken covenant. Broken covenant. Broken covenant.
Over and over and over again.
Faithless faithless faithless.
Jeremiah, O Jeremiah,
I've seen how Rembrandt painted you:
your head in your hands, eyes downcast,
shoulders slumped.
God has been in covenant with faithless people.
But in exile they pray for forgiveness,
reminding God who God is:
a God of covenant love
a God of mercy.
They promise to repent.
God responds:
I have loved you
 with an everlasting love;
therefore I have continued
 my faithfulness to you.
The days are surely coming when
I will make a New Covenant
with the house of Israel and
the house of Judah. . . .
I will put my law within them,
and I will write it upon their hearts;
and I will be their God and
they will be my people.
No longer shall they teach one another,
or say to each other, "Know the Lord,"
for they shall all know me,
from the least of them to the greatest,

for I will forgive their iniquity,
and remember their sin no more.

We would see Jesus!
Exactly!
We would see Jesus!
The world had gone after him,
and we would go after him, too.
In our hearts we long to wave
the palm branches, to shout
our Hosannas,
and yet, and yet, and yet . . .
something holds us back.
We have so much to do:
budgets to raise,
programs to start,
meetings to attend,
teachers to find,
new members to attract,
sermons to preach,
music to learn,
dinners to cook,
buildings to maintain,
materials to order . . .
order the flowers,
order the fronds,
answer the phones. . . .
We'll parade later.

The world had gone after him,
even the Pharisees knew it,
but now the parade was over.
The palm branches were no longer waving.

The Hosannas sang only in memory.
We would see Jesus.
The Greeks stood in front of Philip,
asking to see Jesus.
Philip tells Andrew,
and together they tell Jesus.
The world outside of Judaism
is asking to see Jesus.
This was the sign Jesus had
been waiting for!
God had sent Jesus
to all of God's people.

The hour is come
for the Son of Man
to be glorified.
The hour of Christ's death
is nearing.
The hour of our Life
is nearing.

We see the shadow of the Cross;
the angels begin their lamenting.
If we understand, we tremble,
for if we would see Jesus,
we will see God die.
God's New Covenant
embraces this world.
The world has broken covenant
over and over and over again;
the church has broken covenant
over and over and over again,
and yet, and yet, and yet,

something pushes God forward
past broken covenants.
Love so much Love
that God not only is true
to the covenant made
with God's people,
but God also keeps covenant
on behalf of God's people.
Love so much Love
that God climbs upon a cross
and hangs there
even unto death.
The hour of Christ's death
is nearing.
The hour of our Life
is nearing.

That it had to come to this!
That Jesus had to die
in order for us to live!
Just as wheat dies to the earth
and later bears much fruit,
Jesus had to die to the world
that he could live again
    for all of us
that we through him could live.

I had a plant that died one winter.
Because of the ice-covered earth,
I put the plant in the garage,
thinking I would throw it away
when the ice thawed,
wash out the pot, and replant.

When spring came, I went to
the darkness of the garage
and there in the pot
the plant bloomed green.
Resurrection in my face.

We would see Jesus.
Exactly!
In these Lenten days
we would see Jesus,
see who he really is,
see what he is about,
see how we are to follow him.

If we would see Jesus
we would see him praying
with loud cries and tears.
We would hear him say,
Now my soul is troubled . . .
and yet, Jesus is obedient,
faithful even unto death.
If we would see Jesus,
we will see him die.
And if we see Jesus,
we are to follow.
If we follow,
we will die, too,
to our world
of self-centeredness,
and live forever
in this New Covenant
together feeding his sheep,

God's Love written
upon our hearts.

But there's something terribly wrong!
The world says Hate
when Jesus says Love.
The world says War
when Jesus says Peace.
The world says Mine
when Jesus says Share.
The world says Torture
when Jesus says Mercy.
The world says Kill
when Jesus says Life Abundant.
The world says Do What You Can Get Away With
when Jesus says Justice.
The world says Take Care of Number One
when Jesus says Care for the Least of These.

Oh, we would see Jesus!
But something is terribly wrong.
The church reflects the world.
Shouldn't it be the other way around?
Shouldn't the world reflect the church?
In the Lenten quiet,
we hear the world outside
asking to see Jesus.
It's a sign, of course.
Jesus was sent for all the world.
They would see Jesus.
We live in hope.

Hope that we in the Church of Jesus Christ
one day will step outside our doors
and put our arms around
this cold and shivering world
and in one voice shout:
Love
and Peace
and Share
and Mercy
and Life Abundant
and Justice
and when you have done it unto the least of these
you have done it unto me.

We would see Jesus.

The Anointed One
Mark 14:1–15

The sound of Hosannas still sings in our ears!
The laughter of the crowd,
so excited,
so filled with passion,
so uncommonly joyous,
for it is the Messiah who rides the donkey
just as Zechariah had said:
> "Shout loud, O daughter Jerusalem!
> Lo, your king comes to you;
> triumphant and victorious is he,
> humble and riding on a donkey . . .
> and he shall command peace to the nations!"
Palm branches waving,
coats thrown on the ground in front of him,
this One who comes in the name of God,
this Jesus who comes to save.
Oh, how we love a parade!
Oh, how we love this Jesus!
What then happened?
What did he do?
What did he say
to cause such wrath?

What strange stories:
a hungry Jesus curses a fig tree
because it bears no fruit.
Where, O Israel, is the fruit of your faith?
Where are those who have kept covenant?
Where are those who have walked with God
in justice and mercy and humility?

An angry Jesus drives the
moneychangers out of the temple.
He who entered Jerusalem
in the name of God
has judged the church to be
hypocritical and worldly,
anything but a house of prayer.
"Is it not written:
'My house shall be called a house of prayer for all
     the nations'?"
Open, open, open the church doors!!!
for all who want to kneel in prayer.
Who is this Jesus anyway?
The State and the Church were unhappy,
for he spoke as one in authority and he had
captured the imagination of the people.
Unhappy, yes, but unhappy enough
to plot to kill him?
Jesus told the people to follow him,
to live in covenant with God,
Love God with all your whole being
and and and
Love your neighbor as yourself.
He quoted Isaiah to them:
     "This people honors me with their lips,
     but their hearts are far from me:
     In vain do they worship me,
     teaching human precepts as doctrines."
He taught the crowds that God loved them.
He told them to walk in God's way,
not the way of the worldly authorities.
He denounced the religious authorities:

"They devour widows' houses and
     for the sake of appearance say long prayers."
He told the people to care for the poor,
to visit the prisoners, to heal the sick, even on the
Sabbath. . . .
Is it any wonder they killed him?

And there is always a Judas!
Always someone who will sell his soul
for a little money.
Always someone willing to betray!
And so the end begins.
Jesus had been anointed
by the woman with the alabaster jar,
the woman who walked in Hosannas.
The Passover preparations had been made.
The twelve came with Jesus when it was evening,
and sitting at the table eating,
Jesus told them that
one of them would betray him.
Had we been there,
we would have said
what they said:
Surely not I!
Those eyes looking at each of them:
It is one of you . . .
one who is dipping bread in the bowl with me.
Surely not I!
Surely not I!

This is my body broken for you.
They ate the bread broken for them.
Just as we do.

This is my blood of the covenant.
They drank from the cup poured for them.
Just as we do.
After they sang a hymn
they went out to the Mount of Olives,
and Jesus told them
they would all desert him.
Just as we do.
"I will strike the shepherd
and the sheep will scatter."
Then here comes Peter,
as we knew he would:

> "Even though all become deserters,
> I will not."

Oh, Peter, Peter, Peter,
you are the Rock on which
his Church was built.
It is our voices we hear:
We will not! We will not! We will not!
After all, we've learned from Peter.
We even feel a little sorry for him,
put in a situation like that.
Jesus speaks again:

> "Truly I tell you, this day, this very night,
> before the cock crows twice,
> you will deny me three times."

Even though I must die with you,
I will not deny you!
The rest said the same thing.
But they could not stay awake
while he prayed in Gethsemane . . .
not even for one hour.

And then a kiss . . .
a betrayer's kiss.
Jesus is arrested and
taken to the high priest
where all the chief priests, the elders,
and the scribes had gathered.
Blasphemy!
Condemn him!
Agreed!
Done!
Death!

We sit on the church steps,
our palm fronds in our hands,
remembering our Lenten days.
We would see Jesus. . . .
We had waved our palm fronds
as we paraded into the sanctuary.
Where was the excitement?
the passion?
the uncommon joy?
Instead there is dread and fear,
uncertainty and confusion.
Who do we say that he is?
The Lenten days went too quickly,
as we feared they would.
Are we farther down the road of faith?
Or did we go in circles?
Follow me, he said,
and we thought we could,
but now we face this week,
this so-called holy week
with unholy trembling.

Surely not I!
we whisper under our breaths,
Surely not I!
And so having supped with him,
we go to pray in Gethsemane.
We pray that we can stay awake
for the hour has come,
and we find ourselves in the courtyard
where we must answer
whether we know him or not.
One by one we will be asked:
Who do you say that I am?
Surely we will not be
the sheep who scatter.
Surely we will not desert him.
Surely not I?
I know him. I know him. I know him.
Surely . . .

Now to Pilate,
who tries to wash his hands
of any responsibility,
What shall I do with this Jesus?
    Crucify him!!
Pilate gives him up to the crowd.
Barabbas is freed.
Jesus is flogged
and crucified.
The Lamb of God is sacrificed
for the ones who deny him.
Surely not I!
Surely not our church!

Surely we know him
Surely . . .
O Lamb of God,
O Bread of Life,
O Light of the World,
O Prince of Peace,
O Bright and Morning Star,
lead us through our lukewarm faith
through the death-shrouded Friday
to the justice and mercy
of your Easter dawning.
May we have the faith to speak
your gospel of life
in this world of death
and the love to live abundantly.
We would see Jesus!

Holy Week

Holy Week

Where have the forty days of Lent gone?
We've had forty days to remember who Jesus is,
Forty days to find out who Jesus is,
Forty days to look and to listen to this man from Nazareth,
this man who walked into the hearts of the people,
this man who "stirred their imagination,"
this man who is still walking into the hearts of his people,
still stirring the imagination of the people,

Holy Week is upon us.
We will raise our palms in joyful recognition!
We do know him.
Surely we do know him. . . .

From Hosanna to Horror, the Only Road to Easter

Balloons maybe.
If Jesus were coming here,
maybe we'd line up on either side of his parade route,
and wave balloons as he passed.
Back and forth . . . a multitude of colors,
and we'd probably shout Yeah! instead of Hosanna,
and we'd hold up homemade posters saying,
  "Welcome, Jesus!"
and as he passed by . . . probably in one of those
  bubble-top cars
because the FBI would not want to be left out of
   this one . . .
On the other hand maybe he'd refuse and ride that
  donkey after all
or maybe even walk down the middle of the road with
  balloons bobbing
as he walked, he'd wave to us and bless us.
And we'd follow, and follow, and follow.
What a celebration! What a Festival of Faith that
  would be!
And when the parade passed by, we'd finally go home,
and look forward to the celebration next Sunday.

But what about Holy Week?
The days lengthen
the pear tree flowers white outside my kitchen
  window. . . .
In the mysterious Lenten mix of lament and hope the
  taunting, blood-splattered
face of war screams into our lives,
and we are tempted to despair.

The TV bleeds and explodes
and the unspeakably obscene inhumanity of war
blares into our ears and our hearts—
and we turn and run.

Into a wall—
the same wall we visit each Lent—
trying to get around a Gate called Truth,
trying to go from Palm Sunday
straight to Easter morning,
trying to keep from going into that courtyard
where we must answer whether we know him or not,
trying to keep from going anywhere near that cross.
So give us the palms and give us a parade,
but O God, whisk us right from Palm Sunday
to that "great getting-up morning."
Have our Easter baskets filled and waiting for us, O God,
because this year we're tired and we're scared
and we just want a little peace and quiet.
And so we turn and run
or we kneel and pray for mercy and for miracles
and the eyes to see this Jesus
named Emmanuel,
the eyes to see that God is with us.

Easter's Morning Light

We Have Seen Jesus
John 20:1–18

O Lamb of God! O Lamb of God! O Lamb of God!
With the slaying of the paschal lambs,
you died upon a tree.
Your sheep scattered
and hid in darkness
weeping.
It was over.

Three days those who loved him
huddled,
their hearts trembling,
their faces swollen from tears.
They would no longer see Jesus.
He himself had said from the cross,
It is finished.
They felt finished, too.

While the early morning
had not yet found its sun,
on that first day of the week,
Mary Magdalene walked
through the darkness
to the tomb
and found the stone rolled away.
She ran and found Peter
and that other disciple
whom Jesus loved.
They have taken Jesus out of the tomb,
she said, and we don't know where to find him.
Peter came into the tomb

and saw the linens lying there,
the head linen rolled up by itself.
Then the other disciple came into the tomb
and he saw and he believed.
He saw and he believed.
We who have sought these Lenten days
to see Jesus . . .
do we see and do we believe?
Who do we say that he is?
He is the one who gathers the children
to himself.
He is the one who speaks with women,
even foreign women, even Gentile women,
even women of the streets.
He is the one who sits down to eat
with tax collectors.
He is the one who eats with sinners.
He is the one who touches lepers.
He is the One.
The disciples went home.
But not Mary . . .
no, not Mary . . .
she stayed,
she wept.
She bent to look into the tomb,
and there she saw two angels,
one at the foot where Jesus had lain
and one at the head.
"Woman," they asked,
"why are you weeping?"
"They have taken away my Lord,
and I do not know where
they have laid him."

I do not know where he is!
Did you not know I would be
about my Father's business?
Who do you say that I am?
Mary said, Rabboni.
Having turned, she saw
whom she believed to be
the gardener,
Woman, why are you weeping?

Whom do you seek?

"Sir, tell me where you have laid him, and
I will take him away."
All Jesus had to say was *"Mary!"*

Mary, Mary, Mary,
Oh, Mary,
Do you not know me?
"Rabboni!"
Yes, she knew him.
She knew Jesus.
She ran to tell the others:
"I have seen Jesus."
And there it is . . .
our Lenten search,
that which we have waited for,
that which we have sought,
that which we have worked for. . . .
He is not some goody-goody god;
he is Justice
he is Mercy
he is Humility

he is Love.
And Mary saw him;
Mary knew him;
Mary followed;
Mary believed;
Mary ran to tell the others.
Later that night,
when the doors were shut,
Jesus came to them
and stood among them
and said, *"Peace be with you"*

as he always did,
and he said it again,
after he had shown them
his hands and his side.

"Peace be with you."

From the beginning
it had been Peace.
It was the song of the angels
in Bethlehem.
It was the song of Jesus,
and Peter preached it to the people:
"You know the message
God sent to the people of Israel,
preaching peace by Jesus Christ.
He is Lord of all."
If we see Jesus,
we know that
he preached peace,
but the thing that's

so hard for us is this:
we do see Jesus,
and we know Mary
and Peter and all the others
believed that we are to
love our neighbors as ourselves,
but that was then and this is now
and it is a different world.
We are a different people.
Can't we disciple in a more
modern way?
Not everyone can preach peace.
Can't we be on the kitchen committee?
Can't we make more rules?
Can't we write a check?
And yet, and yet and yet,
he said, *as God sent me*

I send you.

Receive the Holy Spirit.

He sent them out
just as he sends us out
to all the nations
to tell God's story
of peace and goodwill.

Easter comes.
The shroud that covered
the world is destroyed;
for our God has swallowed death.
We shall no longer look

for him among the dead.
He calls to us to follow,
to believe in our hearts
that the people of this world
will someday love one another.
Really
Love one another.
If we believe we know that
that is not a naive hope,
but God's promise.
We shall not die,
but we will live in him
who died for us.

On Easter morning
and on every morning,
let us in chorus sing:
"This is the day the Lord has made;
Let us rejoice and be glad in it!"
And then with Mary,
let us run to tell the others:
We have seen Jesus!

Catherine's Poem

Eyes believing,
Gifts receiving,
Our hearts can see so many things:
A child in the snow making angel wings,
The grand bravado of marching bands,
An elderly couple holding hands,
The warm sweet silence of the early morn,
A lullaby sung to a precious newborn,
A fire's warmth and a trusting face,
Heartfelt thanks!
Small blessings of grace!

Don's Poem

In retirement he claps his hands at rabbits and squirrels
who nibble at the fruit of his labor,
leaving small holes in the dirt and petals in the grass.
Each day . . .
and yet each day he repairs the damage
and brings me flowers
freshly cut.

Each day God claps for our attention
as we scamper in our destructive ways,
carelessly chipping away at the gifts of God
as though they belong solely to us, and
we can trash this world when we feel like it.
Each day . . .
And yet God repairs and cleans
and brings us new life
freshly born.

I'm reminded of the grace of God
Each day.

Eyes Still Filled

On Tennessee summer evenings
we would lie on our backs,
the stars hanging in our eyes,
and we would wonder . . .
wonder what was going on up there
among the stars. . . .
If we stared long enough,
the stars would lift us to them,
and we would float,
face to face with the stars
in the entranceway of the home of God.
When our mother called us to come in
because of the late hour,
the spell was broken,
and we would fall back to earth,
where our backs itched from the grass
and our thirst was powerful,
but our eyes . . .
our eyes were still filled
with the glory of God.

It's Still about Jesus

No matter how we dilute the word of God,
It's about Jesus.
No matter how we cover the dangerous Truth of the
gospel,
It's about Jesus.
No matter how we pretty up the story,
It's about Jesus.
No matter how many times we go to our national
assemblies and vote,
It's still about Jesus.
No matter how many times we distract ourselves with
meetings
    And church work and the good ole Stewardship
    Campaign,
It's still about Jesus,
Jesus, the Lamb of God,
Jesus, the Light of the world,
Jesus, the Bread of Life,
Jesus, the Prince of Peace,
Jesus, the One chosen to bring good news to the poor,
Jesus, the one sent to proclaim liberty to the captives
    and to set free the oppressed.

Jesus is my shepherd
I shall not
I shall not want.